Henry VIII

Jonathan Melmoth

Designed by Karen Tomlins

History consultant: Kirsten Claiden-Yardley
Reading consultant: Alison Kelly

Tudor Family Tree

(Monarchs of England shown in bold)

Henry VII
1457-1509 — Elizabeth of York

Arthur — Catherine of Aragon | **Henry VIII** **1491-1547** | 2) Anne Boleyn 3) Jane Seymour 4) Anne of Cleves 5) Catherine Howard 6) Catherine Parr | Margaret — James IV of Scotland | Mary — 1) Louis of Franc 2) Duke Suffolk

Philip II of Spain — **Mary I** **1516-1558** | **Elizabeth I** **1533-1603** | **Edward VI** **1537-1553** | James V of Scotland — Mary of Guise | Frances Brandon — Her Grey

Mary, Queen of Scots | **Lady Jane G** **1537-1554**

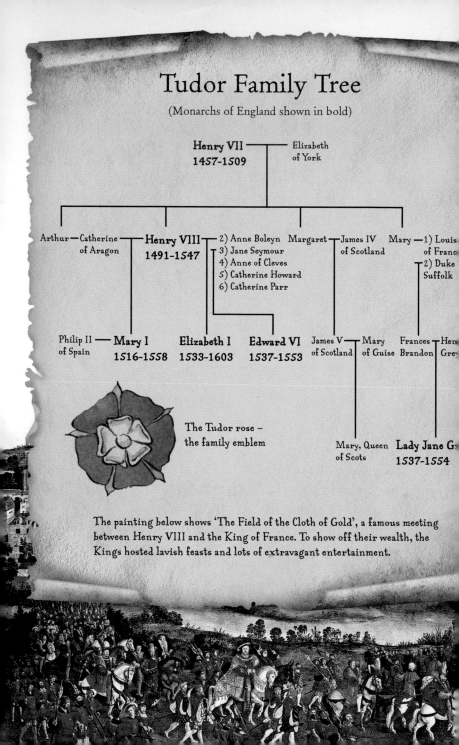

The Tudor rose – the family emblem

The painting below shows 'The Field of the Cloth of Gold', a famous meeting between Henry VIII and the King of France. To show off their wealth, the Kings hosted lavish feasts and lots of extravagant entertainment.

Contents

Chapter 1

A playful prince

"Quickly, Henry!" urged Prince Arthur. "Father wants us all to go to the Tower of London at once. There's been another uprising in Cornwall. We need to be somewhere safe in case the rebels reach London."

It was the summer of 1497. Henry would soon be six years old and his brother Arthur was ten. Their father was King Henry VII, the first king in a new family of English rulers called the Tudors. There

This painting from the 1600s shows Greenwich Palace, where Henry grew up.

were still many people who thought the Tudors weren't the rightful rulers of England, and wanted to replace them. Armed revolts were common.

"If I were King, I wouldn't stand for any of this kind of trouble," said Henry, stoutly.

"There's no chance of that," replied Arthur. As he was the eldest, he would be king after their father died. Henry would just be an ordinary nobleman.

Henry and Arthur spent the next few weeks at the Tower of London, until the danger of the rebellion had passed. Then it was back to their usual home at Greenwich Palace, a magnificent royal house on the banks of the River Thames.

As the King's second son, everyone knew that Henry was unlikely to be king. That meant his father didn't pay too much attention to him while he was growing up. He wasn't expected to behave as impeccably as his brother Arthur, who had to attend royal

Henry as a young boy

events, make friends in the court, and learn how to act like the king he would one day become. Henry was left to learn and play at home, and was hardly ever seen in public.

Life as a young prince was full of comforts, from the finest clothes to the tastiest food. There was no going to school like ordinary boys – instead Henry was taught at home by his mother, his grandmother and a private tutor. But they could be very strict with him, and Henry was a mischievous child, so he had to try hard to be good. He knew that, as a member of the royal family, he couldn't be punished himself – but one of his friends would be punished in his place. So it was best to stay out of trouble.

Henry was a bright boy, and progressed quickly in his studies. He excelled at French and Latin, learned about religion, and also studied subjects such as map-making and astronomy. But what he enjoyed most of all was music. He sang, played the recorder and the keyboard, and even wrote some songs of his own. And when he wasn't playing music himself, he could always summon his minstrels to play for him.

Henry was full of energy, and even music couldn't keep him still for long. He greatly enjoyed playing sports and wrestling with his cousins and friends.

This is a portrait of Arthur, Henry's older brother, wearing a collar decorated with the Tudor Rose.

As Henry grew older, he took lessons in horse riding, archery and jousting – a mock battle in which two knights rode at each other, trying to knock their opponent off their horse with a long pole called a lance.

"When I grow up," he thought, "I'll be as strong and skilled as the best knights in the country. No one will dare to argue with me."

A big public role finally came Henry's way in 1501, when he was ten years old. His brother Arthur married a beautiful Spanish princess called Catherine of Aragon. It was Henry's job to escort the bride to the wedding ceremony at St. Paul's Cathedral in London. Everyone was delighted with the marriage, not least the King, whose idea it had been in the first place.

"Now my family is linked by marriage to the mighty Spanish Empire," he said, proudly. "That makes me more powerful, and enemies will think twice before attacking my lands."

After the wedding, there were eight days of celebrations, with thrilling jousts, huge banquets, and parties all night long. Henry ate until he was bursting and danced to every tune.

Left: This painting from northern Europe shows knights fighting mock battles, similar to those that took place at the wedding celebrations of Prince Arthur and Catherine of Aragon.

But the joy brought by the marriage was not to last long. In March 1502, Arthur fell ill with a fever. He had contracted a terrible disease, for which there was no cure. A few days later, a messenger came to the King in the middle of the night. He brought devastating news: Prince Arthur, aged just 15, had died. The King broke down in tears. He had lost his first son and the heir to the throne, and his carefully made plan to unite England and Spain was ruined.

Henry was now the King's eldest son, so that meant he would take over as king eventually. But the King was troubled at the idea of leaving his kingdom to a young, playful boy. His advisers shared his concerns.

"But he's still such a child!" gasped one.

"I fear he wouldn't rule as sensibly as you," added another. "Can he really be trusted with the future of England?"

"Yes... I believe he can," replied the King, putting aside his doubts. "My son will be the next King of England – King Henry VIII."

King Henry VII

Chapter 2

Hopes and fears

By 1503, the King had given Henry the titles of Duke of Cornwall and Prince of Wales, which gave his young son a taste of his new power and responsibility. Then the King held discussions with Queen Isabella of Spain, to decide what to do about Catherine of Aragon – Prince Arthur's widow. They soon came to an agreement.

"Prince Henry, you are to marry Princess Catherine," announced the King. "When you are a little older, of course," he added, because Henry was only twelve at the time.

Above: King Henry VIII at the age of seventeen

The young prince wasn't sure if he really wanted to marry Catherine, but he knew it was no good arguing. Trying to think like a future king, he also realized that the marriage would be a good move politically. The Tudors would be

Catherine of Aragon

allied to the powerful Spanish royal family again.

But King Henry VII would not live to see the marriage. In 1509 he became ill and died, at the age of 52. He had ruled wisely, keeping England at peace with other countries, raising a stable family, and saving lots of money. No one guessed at the time how different the reign of his son would turn out to be.

The boyish prince, tall and handsome but still just seventeen years old, was now King Henry VIII. He was sad about his father's death, but it was exciting to be King of England. Now he could do whatever he liked, whenever he liked – which for Henry meant lots of jousting, feasting, and going hunting almost every day. He had all the money he needed to spoil himself too, thanks to his father's shrewd, careful rule.

One of Henry VIII's first actions as King was to make Catherine of Aragon his queen. He knew it was an intelligent diplomatic decision, but he was already thinking about something else as well. It was important for him to father a child to take over the throne when he died. It needed to be a son, too, because at the time only men were thought to be strong enough to rule a kingdom. Henry knew that having a baby boy was the best way to secure the future of the Tudor dynasty.

Henry and Catherine were married at a small church ceremony in June 1509. Two weeks later there was a much grander coronation in the vast church

The marriage contract between Henry VIII and Catherine of Aragon

of Westminster Abbey, where they were officially crowned King and Queen. Henry made sure the occasion was very much fit for a king, with a joyous procession through the streets and a grand banquet for all the guests. Everyone was impressed at the new King's generosity, especially Queen Catherine.

"Our time is spent in continuous festival," she wrote in a letter to her father, soon after the wedding.

Even though he was now King, Henry was still a boy at heart. He had little interest in the details of running the country, and left his advisers to organize law-making, tax collection, and other things he found dull. Some people even said that he gave his chief adviser, an influential religious leader called Cardinal Thomas Wolsey, almost as much power as he had himself.

Henry, meanwhile, concentrated on his own interests. He went out on hunt after hunt, and ordered tennis courts to be built at many

King Henry VIII in discussion with Cardinal Wolsey

A game of tennis, as it was played in Tudor times

of his palaces, so he could challenge noblemen to
matches. Such was Henry's enthusiasm for tennis
that it would become a popular pastime for royalty,
later earning the nickname 'the sport of kings'. For
important occasions, the King arranged great jousting
tournaments, with crowds of people invited to attend.
Knights competed at jousting for huge sums of prize
money, and there were parties, shows and feasts every
night. Henry loved to joust himself, and also took
part in events such as wrestling and archery. As he
was tall, strong and athletic, he could easily defeat
most of his competitors. In any case, anyone who
might have been able to beat him was unlikely to try
too hard for fear of embarrassing the King.

Still, while Henry enjoyed the pleasures of jovial parties and sports, he also had far grander ambitions. He knew very well the stories of great wars won by past kings of England and wanted to be remembered for glorious victories too.

He summoned Cardinal Wolsey to advise him.

"Richard the Lionheart – now there was a king," Henry began. "He ruled hundreds of years ago, and people still talk about him because of the great battles he won. Surely I can do something similar?"

"That was long ago – times are different now..." started Wolsey, but the King hadn't finished.

"And what about Henry V? He conquered most of France! Even my own father, Henry VII, will be

This is part of a scroll made during Henry's reign, showing the King and his noblemen on a procession through London. The canopy displays the Tudor Rose.

remembered for winning the battle that brought my family, the Tudors, to the throne. I want a war, Thomas. I *need* a war."

"But wars are expensive," protested Wolsey. "We'd have to pay for a large army, buy them weapons and…"

"SILENCE!" bellowed Henry. "I want to conquer France. Now, make it happen."

Wolsey had to do as Henry asked, and England was soon at war with France. At first, the English armies won some small battles, but the French were well organized and gaining ground against them was hard work. To complicate things further, an army from Scotland attacked England at the same time, and some English soldiers had to be sent north to fight off the invasion.

Henry's military campaigns were failing, and his plans for starting a family weren't going exactly as he had hoped, either. Catherine had twice become pregnant, but sadly both babies had died before they were born. Finally, in 1516, the Queen gave birth to a healthy child.

"At last, you have an heir, my dear," said Catherine, gazing lovingly at her little baby daughter.

"A girl?" muttered Henry, in disbelief. "We'll call her Mary," he added. "The next one will be a boy, I'm sure."

As Princess Mary grew up, she was loved dearly by her mother, and Henry grew fond of her too. She was well-behaved and very religious, which pleased her parents greatly. Henry and Catherine, along with almost everyone else, followed the Catholic religion. But there was a growing group of people who disliked the Catholic Church because they thought the priests in charge were corrupt and dishonest. They began to protest against the Catholic Church, so they would later become known as Protestants.

Henry stuck to his beliefs. He even wrote a book called *Defence of the Seven Sacraments*, defending the Catholic religion. It made him very popular with the Pope, who led the Church from Rome.

It wasn't long before Henry would call on the Pope's support in return. Time went by, and he and Catherine didn't have another child. Henry started to suspect the problem lay with Catherine. She was over 30 years old by this time, which was considered old for

A portrait of Henry painted in 1529 when he was 38 years old

having children in those days. Besides, Henry didn't think she was as pretty as she had been. He began to consider separating from Catherine, but he knew that divorce was very uncommon, even for royalty. If he wanted a divorce, he would need special permission from the Pope himself.

Then, to complicate matters further, someone arrived in London who would change the course of his life. She was young, beautiful, and already had the elegance and grace of a queen. Henry fell madly in love. Her name was Anne Boleyn.

Chapter 3

The King's Great Matter

Anne Boleyn had moved to London in 1522, after growing up in various different parts of Europe. Her father, a successful politician, had arranged for her to become a lady-in-waiting to Catherine, which meant that she would accompany the Queen to social events and assist with day-to-day duties. He hoped this position would help her to meet a wealthy, influential man to marry. He little realized, however, just how wealthy and influential a man she would find.

Above: Anne Boleyn

Anne was elegant, well-mannered and very beautiful, so it wasn't long before she had a number of admirers at court. Among them was the King himself. When Henry set his heart on something, he did everything in his power to get it. He showered Anne with gifts of precious jewels and fine clothes, and wooed her with romantic love-letters. The more he saw of her, the more he longed for her. However, Anne was a strong, determined woman and she wasn't going to settle for anything less than marriage.

"If you really love me, you'll make me your queen," she told Henry firmly.

Henry knew that he couldn't make Anne his wife as long as he was married to Catherine, but the Pope had already written to say that Henry wasn't allowed a divorce. The King wasn't going to give up easily, though. He asked the Pope to send a representative to England, hoping that he would have more success presenting his argument in person.

An ambassador called Cardinal Campeggio came to London on behalf of the Pope. Day after day, he had heated discussions with Wolsey, the King's chosen negotiator, at an official court hearing of Henry's case. But the Pope had told Campeggio not

Catherine being questioned by Cardinal Wolsey, with
Cardinal Campeggio (far right) listening intently

to budge. Months later, the divorce had still not been
agreed, and Campeggio returned to Rome. Now,
Wolsey was left with the tricky task of explaining to
the King why he hadn't succeeded.

"It was a hopeless task, Your Majesty. Queen
Catherine's family is very powerful in Europe. Neither
Campeggio nor the Pope want to upset them..."

"USELESS! Get out of my sight!" thundered the
King. "If you can't do your job properly, I'll find
someone else who can."

Henry wasn't about to let anyone stand in his way,
especially on something so important. By this time,
everyone knew how desperately he wanted to marry

Anne and have a son with her. It became known as 'The King's Great Matter'.

Soon, Wolsey was dismissed and replaced by another adviser, Sir Thomas More.

"Listen," the King told his new right-hand man, "It must be God's will that Catherine hasn't given birth to a healthy son for me. He is upset at the marriage."

"I know what you're trying to suggest," replied More. "You think that God isn't happy about you marrying your brother's widow, so He's stopping you from having a son…"

"Exactly!" encouraged Henry.

"…but I'm afraid I don't agree," added More, gravely. "And in any case, I can't disobey the Pope. His decision is final."

"If the Pope won't give me what I want, I'll have to take matters into my own hands," Henry decided.

His first step was to turn Catherine out of her royal residence and invite Anne Boleyn to move in instead. Then, he consulted the country's best scholars and most famous lawyers. He asked them to scour religious and legal documents to find something – anything – he could use to justify the divorce.

"Sire," reported the head of the investigation, "we may have found a way. As you know, the reason you need the Pope's permission is because he's in charge of the Catholic Church for the entire world, including England."

"Yes," replied Henry, gloomily. "If only there were a new Church just for England, with a new head who would allow me to do whatever I liked..."

"Precisely," agreed the scholar. "You could create that Church, and call it the Church of England. Then you could put yourself in charge. That way you wouldn't need the Pope's permission to do anything."

Henry turned the idea over in his head. He'd been a loyal Catholic all his life, and he didn't want to defy the Pope unless he had to. But the more he saw of Anne, the more besotted he became. In private, he pledged himself to her, swearing on the Bible that he would find a way to marry her.

Then, in 1533, Anne became pregnant with the King's child. Now Henry had to take action, and fast. Without the Pope's permission, he married Anne Boleyn in a small, secret ceremony attended by only a few of his closest supporters. He had defied the Pope, and now there was no going back.

In this painting, Anne Boleyn is shown with the lute she played for Henry. Queen Catherine is watching on from the doorway.

When he consulted his advisers on what to do next, they urged him to go on the attack.

"It's time to break away from the Pope altogether," said one of them, Thomas Cromwell, flatly. "Make yourself the Supreme Head of the Church in England. Then you will have complete authority over the whole country, including the churchmen."

By this time, the King was ready to agree to the plan. New laws were drawn up under Cromwell's watchful eye, establishing a new Church of England, with Henry as its Supreme Head. The English people, including all churchmen, would have to swear to obey Henry, even ahead of the Pope.

To make his new marriage lawful, he needed the

25

help of Thomas Cranmer – the Archbishop of Canterbury and the most important religious figure in the country. Cranmer had sworn to serve the Pope, but Henry promised him more power in exchange for his assistance. The Archbishop was an ambitious man, and he eagerly agreed. He cancelled Henry's marriage to Catherine, and a few days later, publicly announced that Henry's marriage to Anne was valid. On June 1, 1533, Anne Boleyn was officially crowned Henry's new queen in a magnificent ceremony at Westminster Abbey.

The royal baby was born in the autumn of the same year. But again it wasn't quite what the King had hoped for.

"Maybe we could call her Elizabeth?" said Anne, standing with her husband over their new daughter.

Anne Boleyn's coronation at Westminster Abbey

"Very well," said Henry, failing to hide his disappointment. "And we must hope for a son next time."

But while Henry now had the new queen he craved, his actions had made him very unpopular. The divorce was a scandal, and up and down the country there was anger that the King had cast off Queen Catherine, the mother of Princess Mary. On top of this, the new laws making Henry the Head of the Church of England upset many people — especially the churchmen, who were outraged that the King had betrayed the Pope.

Those who refused to show their support for Henry quickly learned that it was a mistake. One of them was Sir Thomas More. He resigned from his position serving the King because he didn't agree with the divorce. But even then he wasn't safe.

"Come on More, you must sign it," demanded Cromwell, as he pushed a document in front of the old man. It was another new law, the Act of Succession, which made Princess Elizabeth heir to the throne instead of Princess Mary. "If you don't sign, you'll be charged with treason," he added, holding out the quill pen.

"No," said More, defiantly. "This is a step too far."

Thomas More says goodbye to his daughter for the last time, as he is taken away to the Tower of London.

More didn't last long after that. He was sentenced to death and beheaded at the Tower of London. Anyone else who didn't agree with one of the King's new laws met the same fate.

Through brute force and determination, Henry had managed to get his own way despite opposition from the Pope and the English people. In Thomas Cromwell, he had a clever and loyal servant to help him rule. Still, what he wanted most was a son to be his heir. Luckily, it wasn't long before Anne was pregnant again.

"This time it must be a boy!" said Henry cheerfully. "What do you think, Anne – shall we call him Edward, or Henry?"

Chapter 4

Anne's fate

Henry and Anne were happy together, not least because they had the birth of a new child to look forward to. They spent vast amounts of money on refurbishing grand palaces to their extravagant tastes, and Henry enjoyed spoiling his queen with glittering jewels and fine gowns. But if he thought Anne would be happy to play the role of an obedient wife and mother, he was wrong. Anne was bold and determined, and wasn't afraid to speak up against her husband, or indeed anyone else who disagreed with her.

"I am the Queen of England, and I will do as I please," she declared, haughtily.

Anne began to interfere with political matters, and upset some of Henry's most powerful advisers by telling them what to do. The truth was, they didn't like the fact that she was so sharp and intelligent, but being a woman made things even worse.

"Women should do as they're told," they grumbled. "If the King wasn't so besotted with

Queen Anne, we'd get rid of her in an instant."

Unfortunately for Anne, Henry was losing patience with her too.

"She should learn to control that fiery temper of hers," he told Cromwell in private. "If only she was more like her new lady-in-waiting – the quiet one – what's she called again?"

"Jane Seymour, Your Majesty?" offered Cromwell.

"Yes, that's right. A pretty young thing, and so quiet and respectful, too. Still, at least Anne will soon give me a son," said Henry, although his mind was already wandering to Jane Seymour.

But the King little knew the trouble he would soon be facing. In January 1536, with the birth of their new child just a few months away, Henry organized a jousting tournament.

"Must you take part yourself?" asked Anne, as he left the palace. "Jousting is very dangerous, and you are the King after all."

"Exactly," replied Henry. "A good king leads by example. Besides, you know how much I enjoy it."

At the tournament, Henry's servants helped him into his full suit of battle gear and hoisted him onto his horse, which was also clad in thick sheets of protective metal. But as the King rode towards the

This portrait of Henry at the age of 36 was painted by the King's Painter, Hans Holbein. Henry commissioned it to show him looking confident and imposing.

jousting arena, his horse suddenly reared up and threw him to the ground. Then it fell straight down on top of Henry, crushing him under its full weight.

Servants rushed over to find Henry lying motionless on the ground. The cry went around: "The King is dying!"

Henry VIII's jousting gear

For two long hours Henry lay as still as death, knocked unconscious by the impact. A messenger was sent to give the bad news to the Queen.

"The King has had an accident," he told her solemnly. "He is unlikely to live to see the sun set."

Finally, just as people had given up hope, the King woke with a start.

"My leg!" he groaned.

Henry was alive, but he was badly hurt. Although doctors assured him that his leg would heal quickly, it never did. The injury stopped him from playing most of his beloved sports ever again, and he had difficulty walking for the rest of his life.

Meanwhile, Anne was badly shaken by Henry's brush with death. She cared for him as her husband and the father of her daughter Elizabeth – but she also knew that if he died she would be in grave danger. Without Henry's protection, her enemies at court would turn on her in an instant. But even with his support, Anne was now all too aware that she would be in a difficult position if she didn't give him the thing he wanted most – a son. Only as mother to a male heir would Anne be truly secure.

A few weeks later, Anne's worst fears were realized: the baby died before it was born. Anne was distraught, but Henry wasn't in the mood to sympathize. Instead, he called for his trusty adviser, Thomas Cromwell.

"This marriage is cursed!" declared the King. "Why else would God deny me a son? I need a new wife, Cromwell. I want to be rid of Anne."

"Leave it with me," came the reply.

Thomas Cromwell, the King's cunning adviser

Earlier in his career, Cromwell had been a lawyer, and he set about compiling a court case against Anne. It didn't turn out to be very difficult. Anne's strong will and temper had made her so unpopular that there was no shortage of people willing to accuse her of crimes, even though she hadn't committed them.

This 19th-century painting depicts Anne Boleyn being comforted by her sister.

Worse still for Anne, Cromwell was one of the most powerful and feared men in the country. He knew that when the trial began, he could influence the judge and jury.

Soon, Cromwell had stitched together a convincing story. Anne was charged with seeing other men while she was married to Henry, and even plotting to kill the King so that she could marry someone else. With Cromwell presenting the case, it was no surprise when the verdict was delivered: guilty.

The charges were so serious that there could only be one outcome – Anne was sentenced to death.

It was left to Henry to decide how she should be executed.

"Anne has always been a graceful and elegant queen. She should die with dignity, not be burned at the stake," he commanded.

"Beheading, Your Majesty?" asked an assistant.

"Yes, but not with a common axe. Let her die by the sword, in the French manner."

Henry had an expert swordsman brought over from France especially. On May 17, 1536, Anne Boleyn was executed at the Tower of London, with one swift stroke of the sword.

Chapter 5

Triumph and tragedy

If Henry felt any last-minute pang of guilt about getting rid of Anne Boleyn, it didn't take him long to recover. The day after her execution, he was engaged to be married to Jane Seymour. Jane was a quiet, well-mannered girl who had assisted both Henry's previous wives, Catherine and Anne. She wasn't as powerfully connected as Catherine or as intelligent as Anne, but she was kind, obedient and loyal. Henry was so desperate for a son that he couldn't wait to make her his queen. Just ten days later, Henry and Jane were married.

But Henry had more to worry about than just his quest for a male heir. All those extravagant

Jane Seymour

tournaments, generous gifts and wars abroad had cost a large amount of money. The reserves of cash which his father had saved up were almost entirely spent.

"We have to do something to raise funds," Cromwell advised. "At this rate, England will soon run out of money."

Henry demanded answers from his advisers. It wasn't long before they found a way for the King to make large sums of money. Better still, the scheme they came up with would reinforce the religious laws Henry had recently introduced.

The King's advisers pointed out how many monasteries there were around the country. Over centuries, the monasteries had become very wealthy, and now controlled lots of valuable land. The monks and nuns who ran the monasteries were supposed to help the poor, but some people thought that they had become lazy and just lived off their wealth instead.

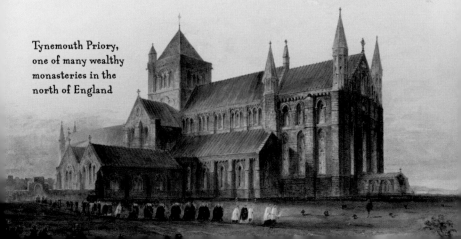

Tynemouth Priory, one of many wealthy monasteries in the north of England

"So, if we get rid of the monasteries…" Henry said as he pondered the plan, "…we can sell off their land to make money. The Pope would be furious, though."

"Exactly," urged Cromwell. "It will help to remind people that you're the Head of the Church in England now."

Henry was convinced, but he wanted to go cautiously at first.

"Cromwell, visit the monasteries and find out how much they are worth and how corrupt the monks and nuns really are. Remember – if we're closing the monasteries, we need a good reason." So Cromwell and his men set about inspecting monasteries all over England and compiling reports. Not surprisingly, the findings didn't reflect well on the monasteries, or on the monks and nuns who lived in them.

"Corrupt. Unlawful. Dishonest," Cromwell reported to the King. "The monks have grown fat on their own success. It's time to get rid of them."

Over the next few years, more than 800 monasteries in England were closed down. Everything they owned was sold, and the money was given to the King. This became known as the Dissolution of the Monasteries.

It was true that some monks and nuns had become greedy, but many people disliked the way Henry was using religious arguments to get what he wanted. There were riots against the King, as people already angry at his treatment of Catherine and Anne finally lost their patience.

HOW HENRY VIII HAD THE MONKS TURNED OUT OF THE MONASTERIES

This drawing shows monks being thrown out and their possessions being taken.

The largest of these uprisings saw thousands of protesters march on the city of York, in the north of England. They took control of the city, and returned monks and nuns to the houses they had been expelled from. This was known as the Pilgrimage of Grace, but it wasn't to last. Henry dispatched a force to crush the revolt, and the rebel leaders were arrested and thrown into jail.

"Now I'll show everyone what happens to people who betray me," said Henry, and ordered them to be hanged, drawn and quartered – a particularly gruesome method of execution reserved for male traitors. Then he had the leaders' heads impaled on wooden spikes and

Traitors' heads on spikes

displayed above London Bridge to warn people how ruthless their king could be.

Henry may have been struggling to keep control of his country, but his family life was going much more to his liking. Jane was expecting a baby. After so many misfortunes in the past, Henry wanted to make sure she was looked after in every possible way.

Jane was excused from all her royal duties, and spent her days relaxing at the magnificent Hampton Court Palace. Her every wish was catered for, even when she

Hampton Court Palace as it looks today

asked for something unexpected.

"Oh, how I crave quail to eat! What funny things this child makes me feel," she remarked to Henry.

Henry promptly ordered a special delivery of the small birds from France.

"My queen, carrying my child, will want for nothing," he said, proudly.

When the time came, the very best midwives and doctors were summoned, and Jane retired to her rooms to give birth. Henry waited anxiously for news. Finally, after two whole days, the child was born.

"A boy at last!" Henry exclaimed in delight. "He shall be called Edward."

Sadly, the joy of having a son came at a great cost. During the birth, Jane became ill, and she died a few days later. Henry was devastated. He had been happier than ever before with the kind and caring Jane. She had given him the healthy son he'd wanted for so long, and secured a lasting place in his heart.

Chapter 6

Trials and errors

After Edward's birth and the death of his beloved Jane, Henry was in no mood to remarry – at least not right away. Instead, he concentrated on improving England's military strength. He wanted to be able to invade other countries, but he was also wary of enemy attacks. His divorce from Catherine and split from the Pope had made him very unpopular in Catholic countries, and he feared

Above: King Henry in the royal nursery, giving Edward a toy ship

that they might form an alliance against England. Henry had always wanted his country to have a commanding presence, especially at sea.

"Britain is an island, so England must have a great navy," he reasoned.

Earlier in his reign, he had ordered huge investments in shipbuilding. The British fleet now had more than 30 ships, including a mighty warship, the *Mary Rose*. Armed with the most powerful cannons of the time and carrying up to 700 men, it was capable of sinking an enemy ship in a matter of minutes.

This is one of Henry's formidable new ships, the *Henri Grace à Dieu*.

As well as strengthening his navy, Henry decided to build a series of imposing fortresses along the coast, to deter attacks from the sea. The forts were paid for with money from the Dissolution of the Monasteries – some of them were even built out of the very stone taken from the monasteries.

Still England was not secure enough for the King's, or Cromwell's, liking.

"Why not marry again, perhaps a foreign princess from a powerful royal family?" urged Cromwell. "That would ensure we had the support of at least one other country if an alliance of Catholic countries formed against us."

One of the stone fortresses built to protect England's coast

"A very sensible idea as usual, Thomas," Henry agreed. "The question is: who?"

"There are two unmarried sisters from the family that rules the Duchy of Cleves," Cromwell suggested. Cleves was a powerful state in a part of northern Europe called Flanders. "Their brother is the Duke of Cleves himself, and he too has rejected the Pope's authority," continued Cromwell.

"Then we would make well-suited allies," agreed Henry. A wife of Henry's had to be more than just well-connected, though. "Have an artist go to Cleves and paint portraits of the sisters, and I shall marry the more beautiful one," he demanded.

The King's Painter, Hans Holbein, went to Cleves and returned with his paintings.

"How delightful!" announced Henry, pointing at the portrait of the elder sister, Anne of Cleves. "Cromwell – arrange for us to be married as soon as possible."

So Cromwell went away and negotiated a marriage contract with the Duke of Cleves. A few months later the marriage was agreed, and arrangements were made to bring Anne to England.

However, when she arrived in December 1540, things didn't go well. Henry visited Anne as a

Hans Holbein's painting of Anne of Cleves

surprise, but when a fat middle-aged man appeared at the door of her chamber, Anne didn't recognize him as the King and paid him little attention. Henry was offended, and his pride was hurt.

Unfortunately, this uneasy start was a sign of things to come. Anne was well-educated and very polite, but she was too sensible for the King's taste. She wouldn't take part in the games Henry loved, and sat solemnly through parties instead of joining in with the merriment.

Henry had soon had enough.

"I don't like her!" he told his advisers. "She's dull and old and…and…she smells strange."

He ordered Cromwell to cancel the agreement with Cleves, but it was already too late. He had signed the marriage contract, and try as he might, there was no wriggling out of it. Henry and Anne were married a few days later, much to the King's displeasure.

Henry soon made his feelings clear to his new queen, and demanded an immediate divorce. Anne knew all too well what had happened to earlier queens who got on the wrong side of Henry. Sensibly, she agreed, and they separated officially just a few months later. As a reward for going along with the divorce, Henry gave Anne several palaces where she could live out the rest of her days in peace. They even became good friends in later life, and Anne was referred to as 'the King's beloved sister'.

Despite having managed a quick escape from his latest marriage, Henry was still embarrassed by the whole episode. He needed someone to blame. Inevitably, his anger turned to Cromwell, who had arranged the ill-fated match in the first place. For many years, Cromwell had ruthlessly disposed of any rivals to protect his own power at court. Now it was his turn to be disposed of. On the King's orders, Cromwell was thrown into the Tower of London, and executed in July 1540.

The King, meanwhile, had already found a new object for his affections – a girl named Catherine Howard. She was young, pretty and enjoyed being the focus of attention, especially when powerful

Catherine Howard

men were around. Her charms certainly worked on Henry. He was soon infatuated by the girl he called 'a rose without a thorn', and wooed her with gifts of land and expensive jewels. Within weeks of the end of his fourth marriage, Henry was engaged again.

The wedding took place that same year, but again the marriage would not last for long. Soon, there was talk that, before she met Henry, Catherine had been engaged to marry a man named Francis Dereham. If it was true, the King's marriage to Catherine would be unlawful. There would be a scandal, and the King would look like a fool.

Thomas Cranmer, the hard-hearted Archbishop of Canterbury, took it upon himself to investigate. He already disliked Catherine's family, and was quick to seize upon the chance to destroy her marriage to Henry. He questioned the Queen rigorously about

Thomas Cranmer

Dereham. Then he quizzed her servants, keeping his ears pricked for any gossip he could use against their mistress. Over the course of the interviews, the name of another handsome young courtier kept cropping up – Thomas Culpeper. It seemed that Catherine had been meeting with him behind the King's back. Then, Cranmer found a letter written by Catherine to Culpeper after she became Queen. It contained enough evidence for Cranmer to claim that Catherine had acted dishonestly.

"I never longed so much for a thing as I do to see you and to speak with you," she had written.

Cranmer told the King about Catherine and Culpeper, as well as her past relationship with Dereham. The King was devastated, and furious.

Catherine was stripped of her title and sent to Syon House, a former monastery outside London,

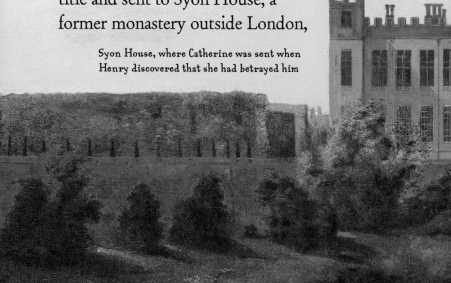

Syon House, where Catherine was sent when Henry discovered that she had betrayed him

where she was kept under guard. Culpeper and Dereham were arrested and thrown into jail at the Tower of London. They were tortured and asked again and again to confess their crimes. Finally, Culpeper gave in and admitted to meeting the Queen in secret, and Dereham accepted that he had once wanted to marry Catherine. Both men were sentenced to death and executed a few days later.

With their confessions, Catherine's fate was sealed, too. By the time the King's guards escorted her along the River Thames and into the Tower of London, she could see the heads of Culpeper and Dereham impaled on spikes above London Bridge. On a cold winter's morning in February 1542, Catherine Howard was beheaded. She was just 21 years old.

Chapter 7

A fat old king

After years of personal and political struggle, Henry had become more bitter and ill-tempered than ever. He still had the mind of a bold young king, but he was now 50 years old, and extremely fat. Stubborn injuries and illnesses made his body weak with aches and pains, but still he ruled his subjects with such authority that nobody dared to defy him.

In 1543 he was married again, this time to a wealthy widow named Catherine Parr. She was a dignified, caring woman who made a reliable companion for Henry in his later years. She looked

after his children, helping to educate them, and even persuaded Henry to reinstate Mary and Elizabeth as heirs to the throne. Of course, Prince Edward, as Henry's only

Left: Catherine Parr

Right: A portrait of Henry VIII in 1542

son, was still first in line to become the next King, but it meant that if anything happened to Edward, Mary or Elizabeth might one day rule in his place.

Henry knew that he was coming towards the end of his life, and it made him even more determined to win great victories for England while he still could. He invaded Scotland again, hoping to conquer it once and for all. Henry realized the Scots would fight ferociously to protect their freedom, though. It was clear that even if they were defeated on the battlefield, they wouldn't give in and accept English rule.

So, after a crushing English victory at the Battle of Solway Moss, Henry decided to try a different tactic. He forced the Scottish lords to agree to a future marriage between Prince Edward and Mary, Queen of Scots, who was only a baby at the time. In return, Henry would stop attacking Scotland.

The King's plan was to use the marriage to unite the kingdoms of England and Scotland. England was larger and more powerful, so the English king would hold all the real power, he thought.

This painting was commissioned by Henry to celebrate his decision to restore his daughters to the succession. Mary is on the far left and Elizabeth on the far right. Prince Edward is shown standing with his father and mother, Jane Seymour, even though she had died years earlier.

Although the Scots signed the agreement to buy some time, they were wise enough to see where it would lead. As soon as their army had regrouped, they broke the treaty. This sparked many more years of war between the two countries, known as the Rough Wooing, in which Henry tried to defeat the Scots so that he could force Mary to marry Prince Edward. English armies were sent to destroy towns and cities across southern Scotland. They even burned the Scottish capital city, Edinburgh, to the ground.

A drawing made at the time, showing Henry's army entering the city of Edinburgh

But Scotland would not submit. It had support from England's other old enemy, France. The French made an alliance with the Scots, and the King of France arranged for his own son to marry the Scottish queen. Henry had been thinking about attacking France anyway, and was never afraid of a fight, so he declared war on the French too. An English army was sent to invade, with Henry anticipating a glorious campaign that would see him conquer large swathes of France.

The war was much harder going than he'd expected, though. English armies fought battle after battle, but only conquered a small area in northern France. When they reached the walled city of Boulogne, they laid siege to it. Henry himself joined his men outside the city, but it was only after months of bombardment that the people inside finally surrendered. The English soldiers who moved into Boulogne were weary, and in no state to carry on. By now, Henry was running out of money to pay his soldiers and equip them with weapons.

To make things worse, the French were fighting back. They sent soldiers to support the Scots, and launched 200 ships to invade England.

Henry scrabbled to defend his kingdom, sending more troops to fight in Scotland, and ships to meet the French fleet at the Battle of the Solent. The English managed to withstand the French attack, but not without great loss. The *Mary Rose*, the King's beloved flagship, sank during the battle, killing almost all of the 400 men who were on board.

Henry had had enough. He offered to withdraw from France, as long as he could keep control of Boulogne. The French king agreed, and the war was over.

Back in London, Henry's health grew worse and worse. The leg wound from his jousting accident all those years before had never healed, and the extra weight he now carried didn't help. His legs were covered in ulcers that oozed pus and had to be dressed by doctors every day. Eventually, the strain on his body took its toll.

A 20th-century painting depicting the *Mary Rose* sinking in the Solent, a channel of water off the south coast of England

For eight days he lay in his chamber at the Palace of Whitehall in Westminster, unable to move from his bed. Finally, on January 28, 1547, Henry VIII died. He was 55 years old.

Henry's will, which confirmed that the throne would pass to his son, Edward

The news was announced, and church bells rang out in mourning across the land. The funeral was a grand occasion, quite suitable for such an extravagant man. The King's huge coffin was draped in golden cloth, and a life-size wax likeness of him, wearing a jewel-studded crown, was placed on top. It needed sixteen strong men to carry Henry to his final resting place in the chapel at Windsor Castle. There, he was placed next to Jane Seymour, his beloved wife who had given birth to his only son. After a turbulent reign spanning 38 years, six marriages and countless scandals and schemes, King Henry VIII lay still at last. He had ruled with such strength and character that he would never be forgotten.

Chapter 8

Henry's legacy

After Henry's death, his son Edward was crowned King. The trouble was, he was only nine years old – much too young to rule on his own. Powerful noblemen were asked to form a council, to take care of the kingdom until the boy became an adult. But, just six years later, King Edward VI fell ill and died himself.

Even in his short rule, he had done his best to continue what his father had begun. As King, he had taken over the title of Supreme Head of the Church of England. However, unlike his father, Edward was a staunch Protestant. He and his council put a great deal of effort into trying to turn the English people from Catholics into Protestants.

King Edward VI

But after Edward, the next in line to the throne was Henry's eldest daughter Mary, a strict Catholic. The ruling council knew that if Mary became Queen then all their work would be undone. They quickly proclaimed Edward's Protestant cousin, Lady Jane Grey, the rightful

Queen Mary I

Queen. But Mary was one step ahead. She gathered her forces and seized the throne for herself. Lady Jane Grey was beheaded, along with her supporters. She had been Queen for just nine days.

Mary began to reverse what Edward had done, forcing Protestants to become Catholic. She proved to be just as ruthless as her father, sentencing anyone who refused her demands to be burned at the stake.

When she died five years later, she had no children to take over the throne, like her brother Edward before her. So, it was now the turn of Henry's second daughter, Elizabeth, to become Queen. Henry had once been so convinced that only men could rule the country that he had Elizabeth's mother, Anne Boleyn, executed in his quest for a son. Yet when Elizabeth did come to the throne, she ruled wisely and fairly – perhaps more so than her father. England thrived during her long and stable reign. Daring explorers brought riches from overseas, glorious victories were won at war, and playhouses up and down the land were filled with joyous music and the famous plays of William Shakespeare.

Elizabeth I died in 1603. She had no children, so the Tudor dynasty finally came to an end.

Queen Elizabeth I

The life of King Henry VIII

1491   Henry is born at Greenwich Palace in London.

1502   Henry's elder brother, Arthur, dies.

1509   Henry is crowned after his father, King Henry VII, dies.
In the same year, Henry marries Catherine of Aragon.

1516   Queen Catherine gives birth to a daughter, Mary, later
Queen Mary I.

1530   Henry's chief adviser, Cardinal Wolsey, dies.

1533   Henry divorces Catherine of Aragon and marries Anne Boleyn.
She gives birth to Henry's second daughter, Elizabeth, later
Queen Elizabeth I.

1534   Henry declares himself Supreme Head of the Church of England.

1535   Henry orders the execution of Sir Thomas More and others who
refuse to accept him as Supreme Head of the Church of England.

1536-41   Henry shuts down monasteries to raise money and strengthen
his grip on the Church. This is known as The Dissolution of the
Monasteries.

1536   Anne Boleyn is executed. Henry marries Jane Seymour. In October,
Henry crushes a large revolt known as the Pilgrimage of Grace.

1537   Jane Seymour gives birth to Edward, later King Edward VI. Jane
dies shortly after the birth.

1540   Henry marries Anne of Cleves. After six months they are divorced,
and Henry marries Catherine Howard. Henry's chief adviser,
Thomas Cromwell, is charged with treason and executed.

1542   Catherine Howard is executed.

1543   Henry marries Catherine Parr, his sixth wife.

1544   England invades France, capturing Boulogne.

1547   Henry dies, aged 55.

ACKNOWLEDGEMENTS

© akg-images p13 (Album/Oronoz). © Alamy Stock Photo p6 (Mary Evans Picture Library), p40 & 41b (Mooch Travel). © The Board of the Trustees of the Armouries II.5/ HIP/Topfoto. © Bridgeman Images Cover (Private Collection/Photo © Philip Mould Ltd, London), p1 (Burghley House Collection, Lincolnshire, UK), p3 (Royal Collection Trust © Her Majesty Queen Elizabeth II, 2015), p4 & 5b (National Trust Photographic Library) p7 (Royal Collection Trust © Her Majesty Queen Elizabeth II, 2015), p8 (British Library, London, UK, Add 24098 f.23v /© British Library Board. All Rights Reserved), p10 (National Portrait Gallery, London, UK/© Stefano Baldini), p11 (© The Berger Collection at the Denver Art Museum, USA), p12 (Universal History Archive/UIG), p14 (© Guildhall Art Gallery, City of London), p15 (Private Collection), p19 (National Portrait Gallery, London, UK/© Stefano Baldini), p20 (Hever Castle, Kent, UK), p22 (Private Collection/ Photo © Peter Nahum at The Leicester Galleries, London), p25 (Private Collection/Photo © Christie's Images), p26 (Private Collection/The Stapleton Collection), p28 (Tower of London, London, UK/Photo © Historic Royal Palaces), p30 (© Walker Art Gallery, National Museums Liverpool), p33 (National Portrait Gallery, London, UK/© Stefano Baldini), p34 (Musée Rolin, Autun, France), p36 (Kunsthistorisches Museum, Vienna, Austria), p37 (Laing Art Gallery, Newcastle-upon-Tyne, UK), p38 (Private Collection/ The Stapleton Collection), p40tr (Private Collection/© Look and Learn), p42 (The Royal Nursery, 1538 (oil on canvas) detail, Stone, Marcus (1840-1921)/FORBES Magazine Collection, New York, USA), p43 (detail) & p44 (Embarkation of Henry VIII (1491-1547) on Board the Henry Grace à Dieu in 1520 /Musée de la Marine, Paris, France), p46 (Private Collection/Photo © Christie's Images), p48 (Private Collection/Photo © Philip Mould Ltd, London), p49 (National Portrait Gallery, London, UK), p50 & 51b (Private Collection/Photo © Christie's Images), p52bl (National Portrait Gallery, London, UK/ Roger-Viollet, Paris), p53 (Castle Howard, North Yorkshire, UK), p54 & 55b (Royal Collection Trust © Her Majesty Queen Elizabeth II, 2015), p58 (National Geographic Creative), p60 (Private Collection / Photo © Boltin Picture Library), p61 (© Isabella Stewart Gardner Museum, Boston, MA, USA), p62 (National Portrait Gallery, London, UK). © The British Library Board p16 & 17b (Additional 22306). Creative Commons p56 Detail from the 'Hertford sketch' of Edinburgh in 1544, by Richard Lee, showing Holyrood Palace. © The National Archives p59 (ref. E 23/4 pt 1 (3)).

Usborne Quicklinks

For links to websites to find out more about Henry VIII, go to the Usborne Quicklinks website at **www.usborne.com/quicklinks** and type in the keywords "Henry VIII".

Please follow the internet safety guidelines at the Usborne Quicklinks website. Usborne Publishing cannot be responsible for any website other than its own.

Edited by Abigail Wheatley and Jane Chisholm
Digital manipulation by Keith Furnival